Raspberry

Raspberry Pi 3 Projects From Beginner to Master Explained Step by Step

John Greenwald

© Copyright 2017 by John Greenwald - All rights reserved.

The following eBook is reproduced below with the goal of providing information that is as accurate and reliable as possible. Regardless, purchasing this eBook can be seen as consent to the fact that both the publisher and the author of this book are in no way experts on the topics discussed within and that any recommendations or suggestions that are made herein are for entertainment purposes only. Professionals should be consulted as needed prior to undertaking any of the action endorsed herein.

This declaration is deemed fair and valid by both the American Bar Association and the Committee of Publishers Association and is legally binding throughout the United States.

Furthermore, the transmission, duplication or reproduction of any of the following work including specific information will be considered an illegal act irrespective of if it is done electronically or in print. This extends to creating a secondary or tertiary copy of the work or a recorded copy and is only allowed with express written consent from the Publisher. All additional right reserved.

The information in the following pages is broadly considered to be a truthful and accurate account of facts and as such any inattention, use or misuse of the information in question by the reader will render any resulting actions solely under their purview. There are no scenarios in which the publisher or the original author of this work can be in any fashion deemed liable for any hardship or damages that may befall them after undertaking information described herein.

Additionally, the information in the following pages is intended only for informational purposes and should thus be thought of as universal. As befitting its nature, it is presented without assurance regarding its prolonged validity or interim quality. Trademarks that are mentioned are done without written consent and can in no way be considered an endorsement from the trademark holder.

CONTENTS

Introduction 1

Chapter One: Building a Classic Game Emulator 4

Chapter Two: Building a NAS with Raspberry Pi 3 12

Chapter Three: Building Your Own Streaming Program with Raspberry Pi 3 23

Chapter Four: Building a Minecraft Server with Your Raspberry Pi 3 Board 36

Chapter Five: Creating a Media Player with RasPlex and Your Raspberry Pi 3 46

Chapter Six: Personal Assistants with Raspberry Pi 3 54

Chapter Seven: Building a Laptop with Raspberry Pi 3 70

Conclusion 79

Introduction

Congratulations on downloading *Raspberry Pi 3* and thank you for doing so.

The following chapters will discuss the projects that you are going to be able to do with Raspberry Pi 3. The Pi 3 board is going to give you the ability to build things that you were not able to before the Pi 3 board came out.

The Pi3 board is the most up to date board that the Raspberry foundation has released and it has the most up to date technology in it. With this board, you are going to have the proper capabilities to become the envy of your neighbors as long as you have the patience and the skillset that is needed to do these projects.

There are plenty of other projects that you are going to be able to do with Raspberry Pi 3, and if you have the knowledge that is required, you are going to be able to create your own project that no one else has created!

There are plenty of works on this topic on the market, thanks again for picking this one! Every attempt was made to ensure it is full of as much useful information as possible; please enjoy!

Note: some of these projects are going to require that you have some sort of prior knowledge of coding with Python. If you do not have this skill, you are either going to need to get someone who does have the knowledge to help you, or you are going to need to learn how to use Python so that you are able to complete that project! You always have the option of looking at the code that someone else has created, however, what they wanted their program to do may not be what you want it to do therefore you are going to have to change their code anyways, which is just going to take more time that you could save by writing out your own code.

Chapter One:

Building a Classic Game Emulator

With the Raspberry Pi 3 board, you are going to be working with a board that has incredible speed and is going to be different to work with than the Raspberry boards that came before it.

One of the things that the board offers you is the choice to turn it into a game emulator that is going to offer you the option to play some of your favorite classic games. And, who does not like to play the classics from time to time? Especially when you are trying to show your kids where their advanced video games came from.

Please note that unless you own a physical copy of the game, you are going to be creating a ROM illegally. Therefore, you are going to want to stick to the games that you own a physical copy of so that you are not putting yourself at risk of being caught and punished by the federal government. This can mean that you are fined or even sent to prison for having an illegal copy of the game.

Before you can begin, you are going to need to gather your equipment. Here is a list of the things that you are going to need to have in order to create your game emulator.

- A game controller with USB connectors
- A Raspberry Pi 3 Model B board
- The proper cables that will allow you to hook your board into the HDMI ports for the TV or monitor that you are going to be playing on.

- A case for your Raspberry board

- Keyboard and mouse that offers you a USB connection

- Micro SD card

- The HDMI cable that you are going to hook into your display device

- A power supply for the board

1. The primary thing that you are going to do is download the retro pie project onto the hard drive of your computer. You will be able to obtain the download file on the retro pie website.

2. At this point, you will need to download another image by the name of Win32DiskImager. After this has been downloaded, you will take the retro pie file

that is on your hard drive and move it to the SD card that you gathered when you were getting all of your equipment together. Before you write the image onto the SD card, you should ensure that you have the details correct so that you are not writing the image somewhere that it does not need to be.

3. Once you have the image written onto the SD card, you will remove that SD card from your computer and put it into your Pi board. From here, you are also going to connect everything to the appropriate ports so that you do not have to do it later on.

4. Your PI should automatically boot up the retro pie. After it has booted up, you are

going to need to press F4 so that you get the command prompt opened on your screen.

5. After the command prompt has opened, you will enter the code: sudo raspi config

6. The expanded file system needs to be selected before you hit accept.

7. Now back to your main screen, you will go to options and locate the SSH option under the advanced options. If it is not already authorized, you will need to enable it.

8. Moving on to overclock, you will choose medium unless you are playing games that have graphics that are more complex, in this case, you are going to pick the higher option.

9. Just like always, you will finish with your options and then reboot your board.

10. After the restart is done, you are going to go to the main screen which is now going to be able to load your game emulators.

11. Your Pi board needs to be connected to your home network, and after you have ensured that it is connected, you will need to go to your network that is located in the windows explorer. There should be a table of devices that are connected to the network, and you will need to go to the one that is labeled RaspberryPi. You will need to double click it.

12. There is going to be a folder titled ROMS, and this is going to be the folder where all

of your games are going to be stored as they pertain to the game emulator.

13. Your ROMS have to be unzipped before you are able to load them where they need to be loaded.

Please remember that if you do not have access to your Raspberry Pi because of the connection that it has to your internet, you can try one of these solutions.

- Take an empty USB drive and plug it into your Raspberry Pi 3 board.

- Wait until the light quits flashing before you pull the USB out of the port on your board and plug it into your machine.

- There should be an empty directory on the USB that is constructed just for the ROM files that you are wanting to play.

- The ROM files that you have unzipped will need to be copied and placed into their appropriate directories on your USB drive.

- Unplug the USB from your computer and plug it back into your Raspberry Pi.

- Once again, wait for the activity light to stop blinking so that you know all of the files have been reproduced over on your Raspberry Pi.

Congratulations! You can now play your classic games with your Raspberry Pi 3!

Chapter Two:

Building a NAS with Raspberry Pi 3

When you are working with various projects and multiple computers, you may discover that you have a bunch of USB disks that you are always working with and probably running into the issue that you are plugging the wrong one in to find what you are looking for. However, there is a way to make the headache go away! You can plug all of them into your Raspberry Pi 3 when you use the board as a NAS (network attached storage).

After you have set the NAS up with Raspberry Pi, then you are going to be able to configure and manage the distro through the browser-based administration interface. It is at this point in time that you are going to be using the

USB ports that are located on your board to insert the USB disks that will be made available on your network for storage. In order to get the best production, you are going to want to use removable disks that are self-powered.

Now, let's look at how this is going to work.

1. Go to the internet and download the OpenMediaVault that is able to be used with the Raspberry Pi board. Your distro is going to have a different release for each of the boards that you can purchase, so ensure that you are downloading the correct one.

2. Now you will take the .img file and move it over to an SD card with the code: sudo dd if = / omv_ 1.17_ rpi _ rpi_ rpi3. Img of = / dev/ sdb. The /dev/sdb needs to be

modified so that it contains the location of your SD card.

3. Boot up your Pi board with the new SD card. There should not be any installation involved which means that you should be able to get straight into the configuration of the distro the minute that it is booted up. Whichever browser-based interface you use needs to be accessed and you need to enter the IP address of your Raspberry Pi 3 board.

4. The program is going make you authenticate who you are, you can either enter the default information, or you have the option of going into your settings and changing the username and password.

5. The system needs to have permission to be able to configure the aspects that are going to be used for the NAS server. This is going to be things such as the date and time that the server is reading as well as enabling plugs ins that need to be kept up to date to ensure that the system is operating on the newest information.

6. Now that your board is up and running as it is supposed to be, you will not need to take one of your USB drives and plugging it into the Raspberry Pi 3 board. You can connect multiple USB if you want to get it all done at once, or you can work with them one at a time.

7. Head over to the menu that is going to handle the storage on your Raspberry Pi,

and select the physical disks option. From here you are going to scan the directories so that OpenMediaVault is enabled and is able to look at the contents of the USB disks.

8. Now you are going to choose the wipe option that is going to go into each of the disks that you have inserted into your Raspberry Pi board and clean them. With OpenMediaVault you also have the option of tying all of the USB together with the RAID software.

9. At this step, you are going to click on the create button, and with the menu that appears, you are going to choose which device it is that you are wanting to be formatted and how you want it to be

formatted. OpenMediaVault supports JFS, XFS, Ext3, and Ext4.

10. You need to go through this method for all of the USBs that you have attached. After you have created the file system, you are going to pick a drive and mount it to your board so that it is now online.

11. You cannot jump right into storing data on your NAS device. First, you have to add users even if you are the only one using the device.

12. You will need to go to the access rights management menu and then move on to the user option.

13. From here you are going to click on the add button which will cause a pull-down menu to appear so that you have the option

of adding individual users or a group of users.

14. It does not matter if you are adding several people at once or a single user, you are going to be adding people to the user's group. Should you decide that a user needs to have their own home directory, you will need to go back into your settings and select the option that allows that user to have their own home directory.

15. The home directory location can also be specified by creating a new folder on the NAS server or by clicking on one that already exists.

16. Here you are going to define a folder that is going to be shared. One thing that you are going to want to keep in mind is how

many users are going to be using the NAS. Should multiple people be using the storage box, then you are going to need to define several different folders for each individual that is using the box so that they have their own folder to be storing things in.

17. In order to add a folder, you have to go back to the access right management settings and then go to the add button once more. You are going to be asked how many people are going to be using the folder and this is where you are going to not only set up the path for your folder, but you are also going to set the backup and the name of the folder so that it can be seen by the appropriate user.

18. In the event that a folder does not already exist, one is going to be created for you. You are going to have the option of adding comments to the folders so that you know what is contained in each folder and you no longer have to search for what it is that you are looking for. Make sure that you are paying special notice to the permissions on each folder. By default, only the administrator of the system is going to be able to access to modify the folders unless they are a user of that folder. Anyone else is only going to be able to see what is in the folder. This is done because it is the safest setting to keep your Raspberry Pi board from being hacked. However, if you are needing to dole out various permissions,

you are going to need to choose this option from the pull-down menu.

19. Even if you leave the default settings on your folders, you are going to be allowed to fine tune those permissions so that a particular set of users does not have the ability to do anything within any given folder.

20. In order to do this, you are going to go to the shared folders option once you have created a user. After going there, you will go to the folder that you are wanting to restrict access to, and you are going to select the privileges button.

21. A new window is going to be opened which will then display all of the users that you have added and what permissions

they have inside of that folder. In order to change what they can do, you will select the tick boxes.

You are now at the step where you can begin to use the NAS storage that you have set up with the network that you are working off of.

Chapter Three:

Building Your Own Streaming Program with Raspberry Pi 3

This is going to be helpful when you find yourself owning an extensive collection of movies, music, and television shows that you have bought over the years. However, because you have so much, you most likely have forgotten what all you own, and it is "collecting dust" on your hard drive.

You can set up a streaming program that is going to be similar to Netflix and Pandora by using the Plex Media Server software that you are going to be able to get for free!

To do this, you will be required to collect these pieces of equipment:

- Your laptop your desktop depending on which one you are wanting to work off of.

- Your Raspberry Pi 3 board

- A micro SD card

- A hard drive that is going to have enough power to support the streaming program that you are creating.

- A power supply for your Pi board. It is recommended that you use a 5V 2A power supply.

- HDMI cable to connect your Pi board to your laptop or desktop.

- A keyboard and mouse for the setup.

- You may also want to look into getting a heat sink for your chips due to the fact that using your board for multimedia consumption is going to cause them to get hot and potentially melt.

- An ethernet cable to access your home network if you are not working off of Wi-Fi.

1. To start, you are going to install the NOOBS operating system off of the foundation's website. You will need to go through an unzipping process that is going to extract the files that you are going to need.

2. Place your SD card into your PC and format it so that it is using the Gnome Disk Utility.

3. Now you are going to need to change the directory that is on your SD card. You are going to do this by inserting this code into the command prompt. Cd/path_ of_ USB.

4. The NOOBS file needs to be unzipped on your SD card; this can be done by using this code: unzip PATH _ OF_ NOOBS

5. It is crucial that you make sure that the contents that are in your NOOBS folder are transferred to the root directory that is on your SD card.

6. At this point in time, you are going to need to plug your mouse, keyboard, and monitor into your Pi board while putting your SD card into the board as well. It is not a bad idea for you to also connect the power supply into the board as well.

7. Your system should automatically start NOOBS so that you are able to install the operating system that you want to use.

You will most likely want to install Raspbian.

8. After the installation is completed, you are going to need to reboot your Raspbian board so that it is now running on the new operating system. All of the files on your system are going to automatically be resized so that they are using the space that is open on the SD card.

9. Using your ethernet cable is going to give you the fastest speed during installation processes, however, you do not have to use it if you do not want to. But, you are going to need to get online with your new operating system and open the command prompt.

10. Enter this code into your command prompt so that you are able to find the IP address that is associated with your Raspberry Pi board. If config

11. After getting your IP address, you will reopen your terminal that is located on your laptop and change the SSH that is on your Pi.

12. By default the password for your Raspberry Pi board is going to be raspberry; however, you can always change this if you are wanting to.

13. Here is where you are going to need to update your system before your next install. It is always best for you to practice with a new distro when it comes to any software installations.

14. After you have updated your board, you will take the external hard drive and plug it into your Pi via one of the USB ports. Your hard drive needs to be formatted to ext4 in order to give you the best compatibility with the Linux system.

15. Now mount your hard drive and make an entry with the fstab so that the hard drive automatically mounts each time that you have to reboot.

16. At this point in time, you are going to install the Plex Media Server. Being that you are using a package that was created by a third party, you need to have their GPG key. For Plex Media, the GPG key is going to be: wget – O – https:// dev2day.

De/ pms/ dev2day- pms. Gpg. Key sudo apt- key- add

17. Your repos also need to be added to the source file. Echo "deb https://dev2day. De/ pms/ jessie main" sudo tee / etc/ apt/ sources. List. d/ pms. List

18. Update your system again so that you are running off of the latest data that is available.

19. Plex Media Server can now be installed with this code. Sudo apt- get install – t jessie plexmediaserver – y

20. After it has installed, you are going to be able to run the service with this code: service plexmediaserver star

That is just the first part of building your own streaming program. At this point in time, you are going to now begin to set up your media server so that you can move your multimedia over to the Raspberry Pi board so that you can stream it without having it sit on your computer taking up space that you could be using for something else.

1. Setting Plex Media up is going to be a simple process, all you are going to be required to do is obey the instructions that appear on your screen. After it has been set up, you will be able to direct the service towards where your media files are in order to move them over. This can be done on any laptop or desktop that is working off of your network. All you are going to

need to do is type the IP address of your Pi board into the web browser.

2. By transcribing the IP address into the browser, you are going to be opening the interface for Plex Media. Plex has a great feature that allows for it to gather information that is located on the internet and taking your media files. But, you need to make sure that you have your media categorized appropriately or else Plex is not going to know that it is a file that it needs to grab. Therefore, you will want to create folders on your hard drive and place all of your multimedia in them. You may want to make folders with names such as "TV shows," "photos," "family videos," etc. Should you move a file into a folder where it does not belong, then Plex is not going to

recognize them, and you are not going to be able to stream them.

3. Now, open the movie tab on your Plex interface and look at the folders that you are going to be allowed to browse. You should select the proper file that is on your hard drive so that they are moved into the new program. Do not rush the program because it is going to need time to scan and process all of the files that you put into it.

4. Not only are you going to be able to access your own multimedia files, but you are also going to be able to locate video channels online. To do this, you are going to go to the channels tab and install the channels that you are going to watch with Plex.

Awesome! You have now put all of your multimedia on Plex! But, how do you access Plex so that you can play that multimedia?

1. Open your browser on the network that you first started working with Plex on and put the IP number of your Raspberry Pi into the URL ribbon.

2. This is going to cause Plex to open automatically. All you are going to need to do is log into the media service and select what it is that you are wanting to watch. Plex also can be modified from the interface that appears on your screen.

3. Before anything appears on your screen, you are going to be asked to set up the Plex Media Player before plugging in the HDMI

cable so that your Raspberry Pi is being displayed here you can see it.

4. To access the contents of Plex on a different network, you have the option of purchasing a PlexPass which will then enable you to stream the content of your Plex account on any apparatus that is connected to the internet. With this, you are also going to be able to share your Plex with your family members.

And there you have it! You have now created your own streaming program!

Chapter Four:

Building a Minecraft Server with Your Raspberry Pi 3 Board

You are able to do virtually anything with your Raspberry Pi 3 board, and you are going to be able to run multiple applications all by using micro SD cards. This includes being able to take the game Minecraft and allowing you to have complete control over the game where you would not be able to if you were playing on a server that is created by the game.

In order to do this, you are going to need:

- A connection to the internet, whether it be ethernet or wireless.

- HDMI cable

- A monitor that supports HDMI

- Micro SD cards

- Power adapter for your Raspberry Pi 3 board

For this tutorial, the NOOBS operating system is going to be used. So, if you do not have this operating system, then you are going to want to download it from the Raspberry foundation website.

1. Once you have downloaded NOOBS, you are going to need to take your SD card and make sure that it is arranged with FAT32. From here, you are going to take the files that are extracted from NOOBS and put them in the root index of the SD card. It is of vital importance that you are not putting everything from the NOOBS folder onto your SD card.

2. With your newly formatted SD card, you are going to need to connect the SD card into your Pi board before taking your HDMI cables along with the mouse and keyboard and plug them in as well so that you are ready to get started with the installation process of NOOBS.

3. After you have downloaded the operating system off of NOOBS, you are going to need to restart your Pi board so that you are running on the new operating system.

4. At this point in time, you will need to connect to your home network. It is suggested that you use an Ethernet cable so that you are getting faster download speeds.

5. Now you will need to update your Pi board so that you can ensure that you are working on the most up to date operating system. Keep in mind that your password is going to be raspberry unless you go to the command prompt and change it to something that is more personal to you.

6. Here is where you are going to be downloading all of the packages that you need to improve your graphics. They are going to come from the OpenGL Driver and you are going to use this code: sudo apt- get -y install xcompmgr libgl1 – mesa- dri && sudo apt – get -y install libalut0 libalut -dev && sudo apt- get -y install mesa- utils

7. After all of the drivers have installed as they are going to need to be opened and

enabled. To do this, you are going to insert code into the same command prompt that you have been using. This time your code is going to be sudo raspbi- config

8. You should see the file system and have the option to expand it or to change the password for it. You are not going to need to worry about either of these options because the NOOBS system is going to instantly expand the file, not to mention that you have already changed the password. Therefore, you are going to skip all of this and go straight to the advanced options button.

9. Once you have gotten into the advanced options, go down to where you see the driver option, select the enter button on

your keyboard before moving over to yes so that the drivers are now enabled. Your mouse is not going to work within these screens, so you are going to need to use the arrow buttons on your keyboard to move around and make your selections.

10. Again, you are going to need to reboot your system and double check that the drivers are enabled. To do this, you will run glxgears in your command terminal, and there should be a little set of gears that appear on your screen that look as if they are turning.

11. At this point in time, you are going to need to get the directories that you are going to be using for Minecraft. You are going to put mkdir – p ~/ Minecraft/Natives into the

command prompt to create the directory, be sure that you are changing that directory to Minecraft so that you know what the file is later on.

12. After you have completed this, you are going to log into your account on the Minecraft website and download the file for the game that is specifically for Linux. This file will need to be placed into the directory that you created for the game.

13. Be sure that you are installing the launcher for the game so that you can log into your account. To do this, you are going to use this code. Java -jar Minecraft. Jar

14. There should be an option entitled "edit profile" and you are going to want to click on that. You should be running on version

1.8.9. If you are not, then select this option from the list and save your profile. In the event that you get an error message, you need to close down the program and run the proper commands to patch the files.

    a. Code 1: cd ~/ Minecraft/natives

Wget https://www.dropbox.com/ s/ 4oxcvz4kyx6f/ liblwjgl. So

Wget https.//www.dropbox.com/ s/ m0r8e01jg2og36z/ libopenal. So

    b. Now you need to update your libraries

Cd/ home/ pi/.minecraft/ libraries/ org/ lwjgl/lwjgl/ lwjgl/ 2.9.4 – nightly – 20150209
rm lwjgl – 2.9.4- nightly- 20150209.jar

Wget https:// www.dropbox.com/s / mj15sz3bub4dmr6/ lwjgl - 2.9.4 - nightly – 20150209. Jar

    c. Next, you are going to need to change the directory to your Minecraft folder. Cd ~/ Minecraft/

    d. Then download the script that is going to be used for running the Minecraft files. Wwget https://www.dropbox.com/ s/ jkhr58apwa7pt1w/run.sh

    e. Ensure that your run script is going to be able to be executed by the program. Sudo chmod +x run. Sh

15. At this point, you should be able to search for the file in your file manager and run it by clicking on it. If this does not work, you

can always run it from the terminal so that Minecraft opens and begins to run on your Raspberry Pi board.

You have done it! You are now going to be able to play Minecraft how you want to by creating the worlds that you want to create as well as inviting your friends to play on the server where you are able to control everything that happens. Use your power wisely! And, never stop trying to create new things with your Raspberry Pi 3 board.

Chapter Five:

Creating a Media Player with RasPlex and Your Raspberry Pi 3

Creating the media player is going to require that you have done the project earlier where you were using Plex Media Server. As long as you have Plex, you are going to be able to build a media player just by using Raspberry Pi 3 and RasPlex. This media service is going to be an open source of Kodi; however, it is not entirely open source.

In order to make this project possible, you need the following equipment.

- Your Raspberry Pi 3 board
- An SD card that is at least eight gigabytes of storage space

- A PC that is running on the Linux system that is going to be used to prepare your SD card

- Keyboard and mouse

- A mobile charger that runs off of a USB cable. It should be at least five volts and two amps.

- A heat sink so that you can control your chips and keep them from getting too hot.

- Your Plex account

- A television that has HDMI capabilities

- An HDMI cable to attach to your television.

1. Take your SD card and plug it into the machine that is running off of the Linux operating system.

2. Go to the Plex website and load the RasPlex installer.

3. Open your terminal and move to the directory where your download is. In many cases, it is going to be in your downloads folder.

4. You will need to make sure that the RasPlex file is executable. You can do this by inputting the following code. Sudo chmod +x getTasplex- Debian 64.1.0.1. bin

5. At this moment in time, you are now going to want to execute the code. Whenever you are putting this code into the command prompt, you do not want to just blindly copy it because the version number for the RasPlex that you are using is going to change, and you need to make sure that

you are using the correct version number or else the file is not going to be able to be executed. Code: sudo ./GetRasplex- Debian 64.1.0.1. bin

6. Here is where your SD card is going to be opened with an SD card writer. You will need to put the SD card into the machine that you are working on if you have not already. Make sure that you tap the refresh button so that the card can be detected by the device.

7. After it has been detected, you will need to choose Raspberry Pi 2 for your model number and select version 1.6.2. Despite the fact that you are using a Raspberry Pi 3 board, the image for Raspberry 2 is still going to work.

8. Now click on download, so the download process begins.

9. As soon as it is done downloading, you are going to write the image onto your SD card.

10. Ensure that you have installed your heat sink because your chips are going to begin to get hot right here as the Pi 3 is working on the HD videos that it is going to be able to play for you. If you skip this step, then you are running the risk of melting your chips which is going to destroy your Pi board and cause you to have to start this entire process over again.

11. Take your Raspberry Pi 3 and plug it into your television by using your HDMI cable. Your keyboard and mouse also need to be plugged in. on top of that, you will need to

ensure that your SD card and power device are connected as well.

12. RasPlex is going to appear on the screen that you are using. Be patient and allow for it to install on the SD card that you are using as well as configure itself.

13. After the configuration process is done, the welcome screen will be displayed which is going to walk you through setting up RasPlex with the setup wizard.

14. In the event that you are using a wireless network, then you are going to need to configure to that network so that you are able to work off of it during your set up process. If you are wanting to change the connection that you have, you will be allowed to do that once the installation has

been completed. You will find this choice in the settings for your system.

15. As soon as you have connected to your Wi-Fi network, you are going to need to log into your Plex account. So that your RasPlex set up is easier, you will need to open up the following URL and get the pin for your RasPlex so that it is automatically connected to your account. (www.plex.tv/pin)

And there you have it! You are now going to be able to enjoy listening to your music on your Raspberry Pi 3! This is going to work on any television that is in your home as long as you have the board connected to your television via an HDMI cable.

If you want to, you can log into the settings for your RasPlex and change them to things such as allowing you to control your RasPlex via a remote control but this is only going to run if you are using a system that allows HDMI- CEC. Even if your television does not support HDMI-CEC, you can download modules that are going to allow for you to use your remote or a keyboard. This makes it much easier when you are having to enter your username and password to log into your Plex account.

Chapter Six:

Personal Assistants with Raspberry Pi 3

Personal assistants are going to come in handy when you are working on multiple projects and need an extra "brain" to help you remember what it is that you are supposed to be doing. The computer that is being coded to be your personal assistant is going to be smarter in some ways than a person is because a computer has more technology at its "fingertips" then a person may. Not to mention, you can talk to your computer and get the information you need without ever having to stop what you were doing.

In order to complete this project, you will need:

- A mouse and keyboard that will attach to your Raspberry Pi 3 board via a USB connector.

- An HDMI cable and a television that supports HDMI.

- A Raspberry Pi 3 board that already has Raspbian Wheezy installed on it.

- Extra wires.

- A Wi-Fi adapter with a USB connection.

- A double pole double thrown relays that runs off of five volts.

- A USB soundcard

- Part of a vero board

- A five-volt power supply

- A five-volt amplifier, you are going to want to keep this small so that it can be held close to your Pi board.

1. Update your Raspberry Pi board; you will need to connect your board to your network via an ethernet cable so that you are getting faster speeds than if you were just working off of a Wi-Fi connection.

2. After you have updated your board, you will need to shut it down so that the new updates are applied.

3. Before using the power back on to your board, you are going to need to connect your Wi-Fi adaptor.

4. Once booted up, go to the desktop and select the option that is going to allow you

to configure your Wi-Fi settings. From here a new window is going to be opened.

5. Select the scan button so that another new window is opened.

6. In this window, you will go to the SSID and double click it.

7. A third window is going to be opened, and you are going to need to enter your password into the PSK box before clicking add.

8. Moving back to the first window that opened, you will be able to check the IP address and see that you are connected to your wireless network.

9. Shut your Pi board down once more.

After you have done that, you are going to be ready to set up the hardware that is associated with creating your personal assistant.

1. Open the plastic case for your sound card; you are going to desolder some of the connectors. You will need to solder where the connectors are so you are not harming the actual sound card components.

2. Taking your DPDT relays, you are going to take the push button on the intercom that you have gotten and connect the DPDT to that button. The second wire that is connected to the switch will need to go into the relay coil while the first wire goes to the ground. This way whenever the button is pushed, you are activating the coil and relay switches. You can also add a

diode in the opposite direction over your two pins that are connected to the coil.

3. The pins that are in the middle of your DPDT relays are going to have a positive and negative connection that is going to go to your speaker. The pins that are usually open are going to be attached to the microphone's input for the soundcard. The pins that are normally closed will be the output of the soundcard. However, you may find that the signal for your output is not going to be loud enough, this is why you need to have your amplifier.

4. Take the five-volt pin for your amplifier and the five volt GND pin and connect them so that you now have power flowing through your amplifier from the

soundcard. You will need to connect the R+ to the R- to the pins that are normally closed in your relay.

5. After you have done this, put everything into the intercom case and then connect your sound card to your Raspberry Pi board.

6. It is not recommended that you try to power everything from your board, that is why you may want to consider getting a three amp wall adapter. Depending on the wall adaptor that you get will depend on if you have to cut the connector to the adaptor and connect a USB connector so that you can power your board.

7. After you have cooked everything up, you will need to close the case for your intercom.

8. Take your sound card and configure it by opening your configuration file. You can do this by putting this code into your command prompt. Sudo nano/ etc/ modprobe. d/alsa- base . conf.

9. The part of your code that says: options snd- usb- audio index = -2 to where it says the same thing except your index is going to be 0.

10. Reboot your Pi board so that the new changes can be applied.

You are now at the point that you are going to be setting up the software that you need to run your voice commands.

1. It is recommended that you use the Steven Hickson voice command software that is going to allow you to have an easy setup and simple to use interface all while being reliable for whatever it is that you are using it for. The software can be located on his website and downloaded for you to use.

2. After you have installed the appropriate voice software, you will input this command. Voice command -s

3. It is with this command that you are going to be able to use the setup wizard and go through it to set up the voice command that is appropriate for your device.

4. After set up you need to enter the voice command -e so that your configure file will open and enable you to set up the

commando's that you need and the actions that are related to it.

5. For configuration you will need to enter the script command = = action it is with this command that you are going to be able to set up the commands that you want your personal assistant to do. So, if you say play, then the program is going to know that you are wanting it to play music. But, if you say something such as play game it will open up your chess game. You will be able to put in any command that you wish to be executed by your personal assistant.

6. After you have completed the editing process for your configuration file, you need to save it. Upon saving, everything is going to be ready for you to use.

7. In order to run the voice command software, you will enter the code voice command-c.

Your personal assistant is now ready to be used! Your personal assistant is going to be able to list to the commands that you give it and execute them appropriately. In the case that your command cannot be executed, then your personal assistant is going to take to the internet and find the answer that you are looking for. Despite the fact that your personal assistant can now execute your voice commands, you are not quite done.

1. You are going to make it to where your voice command starts whenever you launch the program. In order to do this, you are going to go to your Raspberry Pi

home directory and select the configuration directory.

2. Once in this directory, you are going to create a new directory.

3. After it is created, you will need to access this directory.

4. A new file has to be created in the directory with this script. Sudo nano voice command. Desktop

5. Open the file you created and insert the code that is going to cause your voice command to start up whenever you execute the program.

[entry for desktop]

Type = application

Name = voicecommand

Exec = voice command – c

Startupnotify = false

6. Ensure your file has been saved before you reboot your Raspberry Pi 3, board.

Your personal assistant is going to be able to open up programs and gather information from the internet, however, there are going to be times that you want a specific type of information to be returned to you in a particular way. In order to do this, you are going to write out your own script using Python so that you can get this data from the internet and the data that you do not want is not going to even make its way to you due to the fact that it is not what you are looking for.

The biggest issue for this though is that your script is going to be written out and executed as text rather than speech, but there is going to be a script that is going to enable you to have your personal assistant talk to you.

1. The first step that you are going to need to go through is to get a text2speech.sh script. You can find this script online, or you can go to the blog of Oscar Liang and get his script that he has written out to convert text to speech.

2. The script that you choose is going to need to be put into your nano or text editor on your graphics desktop.

3. Just like any piece of code that you put into your Raspberry Pi, you need to ensure that your script is saved and then made so that it is executable. You can do this with the following code.

Chmod +x text2speech .sh

4. By preparing this, you are going to be making the code usable for any applications that have the capability to convert text into speech.

5. The next step is to create the Python script that is going to work with the text to speech script that we have put into our program. For every script that you use, you are going to need to have a corresponding Python script. Your code is going to look something like this.

#!/ bin/ bash

Result = $(python the name of the python script you are using. Py)

./ text2speech. Sh $result

6. This script needs to be saved under any name that you are wanting it to be saved under and then made executable as every bit of code needs to be made.

7. At this point in time, the code that you have written out can now go to your configuration file that you have for your voice command and then any text that is researched by your "personal assistant" is going to be spoken to you in the event that you have inserted the appropriate command.

That is it! Your personal assistant is complete and ready for you to use it.

Chapter Seven:

Building a Laptop with Raspberry Pi 3

With your Raspberry Pi board, you are going to be able to create a small computer that is not only going to be fully functional, but it is also going to run off of the Linux system. With this computer, you are going to be able to do a vast majority of things that a typical computer can do.

Before you start, you will need to assemble this equipment:

- An audio and video output
- Your Raspberry Pi 3 board
- The Linux operating system
- Three USB ports

- A battery that is a thousand milliamp hour with the clamshell case.

- An ethernet cable

- A touchscreen that is about 3.5 inches

- A keyboard

1. You need to make your Raspberry board as thin as you possibly can. This means that you need to take out two of the USB sockets, the connectors for the camera, there are going to be two of them. GPIO pins, the plug for the ethernet cable, the HDMI port, and the jack that is used for the audio and video.

2. Be careful with taking components out of the board because they are not going to be easy to remove. If you damage or scratch

the board, you are going to have to get a new board because the board that you have damaged is not going to work.

3. At this point, you should have a reasonably thin Raspberry Pi 3 board.

4. Make sure that you also take out the pins that are on the PiTFT board. This is going to give you more space and keep it thinner than it was.

5. Here you are going to need to cut some of your wires in an effort to create some extensions that will be used with your ethernet cable, the ports for your audio and video, as well as the USB. You may want to consider tinning the end of the wires because it is going to make working with them a lot easier. Not only that, but

you are going to want to tin the connectors as well so that they are able to be bonded together. You may find that you are going to need to use a stand that frees your hands up so that you are able to use both hands in this process.

6. If you are wanting to make it to where your keyboard powers itself, you will need to get a battery for it. Taking the red and black wires that are connected to that battery, you are going to snip them while being careful not to cut or puncture anything else. If you are using a lipo battery, you are going to want to be especially careful not to damage them because they are very volatile.

7. Here you will have the option of add in a five volt to the regulator on the contacts for the battery. All you need to do is take the red wire and the black wire and place them where they were on the battery. Tinning the end of the wires is going to make the soldering process go much quicker, so keep that in mind.

8. Should you want to, you also have the option of adding a button that turns the backlight on and off for your keyboard; it is not going to matter which color wire you use, you are just going to need to make sure you solder both ends of this button to the contacts. What this is going to do is provide the contacts to come together as soon as you press the button to turn the backlight on or off.

9. Here is where you are going to need to get the case ready for your computer to go into it. You may want to consider using a case that is around two and a half inches. Hard drive enclosures are going to work wonders not to mention they are reasonably cheap.

10. You need to cut and bind the two halves of the case together, this may take some time, but it is going to be best for you to take the time to do it so that you are protecting your Raspberry Pi board as well as the touch screen in the event that something gets dropped on it or you accidentally drop it.

11. You can reduce the height of your power boost by cutting the top of the JST battery

connector in the event that you discover it is too big.

12. Now take everything that you have done outside of the box, and put it into the case. The wires are going to need to be fed between the top and the bottom of the case.

13. Take the time to solder everything together. As for the wires that go to your battery, they need to go through different holes so that you are reducing the risk of your computer shorting out in the event that they break. This is going to look like more wires than you may know what to do with, but all you are doing is taking the extensions and soldering them so that they

are taking the place of the components that you removed from the board.

14. At this point in time, you are going to be able to close your case and attempt to power your computer up.

15. The video from your computer can be outputted so that it is displayed on a television or monitor depending on what you are wanting your image to be displayed on. You are not going to get the best resolution, but it is going to be enough to run videos.

Congratulations, you have now created a computer that fits in your pocket! When you couple this small computer with a touch screen and a windows manager, you are going to be able to free up a bunch of space for other things that you may want to do.

Conclusion

Thank you for making it through to the end of *Raspberry Pi 3*, let's hope it was informative and able to provide you with all of the tools you need to achieve your goals whatever it may be.

The next step is to take the projects that you have now learned how to build and create them!

You are working with technology, and there is going to be a greater risk of messing up; however, you should not let this stop you from proceeding with your project. All you need to do is learn from your mistake and move on because this is going to advance your knowledge of Raspberry Pi 3 as well as the various elements that you are going to be able to do with it.

Hopefully, some of these projects get your creative juices flowing so that you are able to create your own project that someone else may not have thought to build with a Raspberry Pi 3 board. Your projects do not have to be complicated like some of the ones that were described in this book. The more complex that our project is, then the more coding and more time it is going to take for you to put your project together. But, do not let that stop you because you never know who you are going to be able to help by putting your ideas out there for others to see what you have done!

Finally, if you found this book valuable in any way, a review on Amazon is always appreciated!

Thank you and good luck!

CPSIA information can be obtained
at www.ICGtesting.com
Printed in the USA
BVHW081336181120
593625BV00014B/1718